OPPOSITE DAY

Upside-Down Questions to Keep Teenagers Talking and Listening

ZONDERVAN.com/
AUTHORTRACKER
follow your favorite authors

youth
specialties

YOUTH SPECIALTIES

Opposite Day: Upside-Down Questions to Keep Teenagers Talking and Listening
Copyright 2009 by Brooklyn Lindsey

Youth Specialties resources, 1890 Cordell Ct. Ste. 105, El Cajon, CA 92020 are published by Zondervan, 5300 Patterson Ave. SE, Grand Rapids, MI 49530.

ISBN 978-0-310-29278-4

Cover and interior design by SharpSeven Design

Printed in the United States of America

09 10 11 12 13 14 • 20 19 18 17 16 15 14 13 12 11 10 9 8 7 6 5 4 3 2 1

DEDICATION

To all of the people who have been so bold to think and live differently. You have inspired me to try it out for myself.

And to Betsy, Matthew, and Courtney, my sibs, may we share this book with our children and understand them better as we listen.

DEFINITION

OPPOSITE

>   ***ADJECTIVE 1** situated on the other or further side; facing; **2** completely different; **3** being the other of a contrasted pair.
>
>   ***NOUN** an opposite person or thing.
>
>   ***ADVERB** in an opposite position.
>
>   ***PREPOSITION 1** in a position opposite to; **2** co-starring beside.

[Compact Oxford English Dictionary—http://www.askoxford.com/ consise_oed/opposite?view=uk]

TABLE OF CONTENTS

INTRODUCTION
BACKWARD (FORWARD)

A wise and inspired man once wrote, "Do not conform to the pattern of this world, but be transformed by the renewing of your mind" (Romans 12:2). Another translation of these words says, "Don't become so well-adjusted to your culture that you fit into it without even thinking" (*The Message Remix*). These words were meant to inspire a generation of Romans to live differently, to allow a new life with God to shape their thoughts and their actions—and these words are meant for us as well.

I'd like to propose that many of us, when it comes to our conversations, have learned the art of "fitting in without even thinking." We have answers to most questions filed and sequenced, ready for instant use whenever we might need them. But what if you and your group decided to try to listen and speak to each other on a different level? What if you decided you wanted your conversations to be transformed into something more interesting and more revealing?

This is the premise of *Opposite Day*—to evoke a different type of sharing and different responses from each other by using a fun childhood game as our model. This book will get your students talking about things that matter to them by having them share the opposite of what's true. It will be easy to use the prompts found in each chapter to get the conversation flowing.

One purpose of this book is to help you change your "getting to know each other time" in your small group settings. A second purpose is to consider some highly entertaining fictional friends who had some interesting Opposite Day experiences of their own: SpongeBob SquarePants and Mr. George Costanza (of *Seinfeld* fame). To encounter the inspiration firsthand, go to the last chapter of this book, where you'll find two classic television episodes featuring these hilarious characters. They will inspire you and your group to really have fun with these conversations. You may want to jumpstart your opposite brain by beginning with these episodes and end with the beginning of the book. No matter where you end up, it should be easy for you to jump right in and get talking.

Culturally, Opposite Day comes by way of youthful invention and is declared by children on playgrounds or with friends at school. This time, it's up to you when to declare it and when to use it for your small group advantage.

The best outcome of sharing opposites is you'll be thinking and listening differently. You'll get to know each other in an interesting and memorable way.

Each time you use *Opposite Day* to get your group talking, you'll need to explain what the discussion looks like. It's important to explain Opposite Day before you actually start playing the game. Students and leaders alike will find themselves confused and wondering what you mean if you haven't set boundaries. For example, a youth leader could start Opposite Day conversation by setting a cell phone alarm or making an Opposite Day slide to show when the game is live. You might say something like, "In a few moments you or someone in your group will declare Opposite Day." After the declaration has been made, however you would like to make it, your group would begin picking prompts from each chapter to respond to.

To get your mind warmed up, imagine a blatantly guilty criminal sitting in a courtroom awaiting the jury's verdict. Then imagine the representing lawyer declaring Opposite Day right before the jury goes to vote on the verdict. Now that would be smart, but I don't think it would hold up in court.

Imagine going into a bank to pay a hefty debt. Then imagine the teller declaring it Opposite Day, and instead of you forking over the cash, he or she pays you! That would be amazing, and quite possible on Opposite Day.

Imagine the moment immediately before a teenager is to be grounded for doing something ridiculous and irresponsible, but he or she proclaims Opposite Day just before the punishment is given. "You shall sit in the living room and play video games all day until you've not learned a thing, and then you'll be allowed to do your homework." Thank you, Opposite Day!

It would be fun to send out this email to the entire staff at your workplace: "Tomorrow will be declared Opposite Day. Please come in to work whenever you want, bring your children and animals, and don't forget to leave early and take a three-hour lunch."

Opposite Day is a concept for your group to have fun with. Use it wisely, but remember this: If you extend Opposite Day beyond your group time, people who aren't part of your group may get very confused!

Part of the fun in this book is being able to talk about things in imaginative and unrealistic ways. At the same time, by saying what "we're not saying," we'll be revealing bits and pieces of ourselves to each other.

Here's how this should work:

There are opposite chapters to choose from. Each chapter has instructions for you to be able to make the most of your Opposite Day and lists of words or comparisons for you to choose from. There are enough opposites in every chapter for an entire year! But if you're really ambitious you could probably use up quite a few in one meeting.

The words and phrases you'll find are meant to evoke some memory, feeling, or reality for you. Let the first thing that comes to mind be your guide. Therefore, whatever memory, feeling, or reality comes to mind, consider what you would call its opposite. As you share, mask your real responses to the words with things that are just the opposite. For example, if the chapter is "School Opposites" and the phrase is "Book club," I might say something like, "I would probably never belong to a book club, especially one that focused on young adult fiction. I don't really like discussing books with other people." If I heard someone respond like this during Opposite Day, I would guess the person talking might actually enjoy a book club and might also be interested in young adult fiction. Part of the fun of Opposite

Day is in hearing each participant mask his or her reply in the most opposite, over-the-top way possible!

After everyone has had a chance to share and the leader decides to end Opposite Day, it would be good to ask some reflective questions. "What did we learn about each other?" "What new thing did you learn about your friends?" "Did any of your own responses surprise you?"

There are also chapters where you will say what you are really thinking. This will give you a chance to share the truth about different kinds of opposites in your life. For example, you might share about your favorite movie and your least favorite movie.

There is one ground rule in opposite sharing: Share from your heart without hurting others. It would be easy to say something like, "I hate so-and-so," or "I hate this type of thing" (when you really love it). Try to move beyond the word "hate" to reasons why you don't prefer something. I love watching college basketball—especially the playoffs. And I'm not a big fan of watching professional basketball (unless they are in the playoffs). So I might say, "It's no fun to watch playoff basketball." That way I'm not being a hater of the NBA; I'm simply sharing the truth—I only like watching playoff games.

Opposite sharing, like any group discussion, can deteriorate quickly if it's not tended to and guided. Make sure to set boundaries with your students according to their specific needs. Decide whether your group will be allowed to use names of friends when sharing. Take extra time to explain things to younger students. Test out the fun on other adults and work out any fuzzy instructions before meeting with your group. It will pay off with a fun and memorable opening to any group time.

Always give students a chance to pass when asked to share. Never make fun of a student for not getting the concept. Use this book as a tool to help, but try it on another day if it's causing your group to be distracted or frustrated. Ultimately, you know your group best and you have the best insight on how to use this tool.

Now it's time to think opposite.

UNTHINKING | SCHOOL OPPOSITES

IT'S OPPOSITE DAY.

Group leaders, it's time to get the group sharing opposite. After you've explained how sharing opposite works and you've declared it Opposite Day, you'll start the discussion with the words listed in this chapter. Ask each student to respond to the word you provide. Say: "In a sentence or two, tell how you feel about _____ (but not really)." After everyone has had a chance to share, or after a few rounds, you will need to formally end Opposite Day. Be sure to leave a few minutes to share what you learned about each other.

1. Lockers

2. Tardy bells

3. Morning announcements

4. Tryouts

5. Science fair projects

6. Math tests

7. School dances

8. Hall passes

9. Track meets

10. Yearbook pictures

11. Class field trips

12. Cafeteria food

13. Football games

14. Snow or hurricane days (depending on where you live!)

15. Prom

16. Standardized tests

17. AP classes

18. Literature

19. Geometry

20. Take-home tests

21. Bus stops

22. Fight songs

23. Freshman year

24. Study groups

25. Chemistry

26. Senior year

27. Class council

28. Yearbook

29. Physical education

30. Art projects

31. Band practice

32. Basketball games

33. Lacrosse equipment

34. Water polo

35. Wrestling meets

36. Baseball fields

37. Varsity letter jackets

38. Dodgeball tournaments

39. Backpacks

40. Timed mile runs

41. Graduation

42. Summer break

43. Athletic conditioning

44. Class schedules

45. Poetry reading

46. Student government

47. Tornado drills

48. Spring break

49. School musicals

50. Middle school hallways

51. Study period

52. Fundraisers

EFFORTLESS I ROMANCE OPPOSITES

IT'S OPPOSITE DAY.

In this chapter you'll get your group sharing opposite about romance. After you've explained how sharing opposite works and you've declared it Opposite Day, you'll start the discussion with the words listed in this chapter. Ask each student to respond to the word you provide. Say: "In a sentence or two, tell how you feel about _____ (but not really)." After everyone has had a chance to share, or after a few rounds, you will need to formally end Opposite Day. Be sure to leave a few minutes to share what you learned about each other.

1. Secret crush

2. Celebrity obsession

3. Note passing

4. Eye contact

5. "Just friends"

6. Instant messaging

7. Admirer

8. Holding hands

9. *"Public Displays of Affection"*

10. *Hallway glances*

11. *Group dates*

12. *Love songs*

13. *Commitment*

14. *Breakups*

15. Boyfriends

16. Girlfriends

17. Heartbreak

18. Honesty

19. Meeting the parents

20. Awkward silences

21. Song dedications

22. Late-night texting

23. Long-distance relationships

24. The first kiss

25. Saying "I love you"

26. Avoidance

27. Movie tickets

28. Car rides

29. Sunsets

30. Perfume

31. Online game dates

32. Summer love

33. Man spray (I'm talking about cologne, people!)

34. Hanging out

35. Bad breath

36. Birthday presents

37. Chick flicks

38. Boundaries

39. Soundtracks

40. Parties

41. Valentine's Day

42. Curfew

43. Promise rings

44. Campfires

51. *True love*

52. *Forgiveness*

VISITOR I RELATIVE OPPOSITES

IT'S OPPOSITE DAY.

Here's where everyone gets a chance to learn some new things—things surrounding a person's relatives. After you've explained how sharing opposite works and you've declared it Opposite Day, you'll start the discussion with the words listed in the relative chapter. Ask each student to respond to the word you provide. Say: "In a sentence or two, tell how you feel about _____ (but not really)." After everyone has had a chance to share, or after a few rounds, you will need to formally end Opposite Day. Be sure to leave a few minutes to share what you learned about each other.

This is a chapter where things could get personal, especially if a group member isn't happy with his or her family life or needs some encouragement. Be observant as students are sharing and make the call to switch to a different chapter or topic if someone looks or sounds uncomfortable.

1. Loyalty

2. Sibling rivalry

3. Household chores

4. Shared Cell Phone Minutes

5. Cookouts

6. Yard work

7. Vacation

8. Dining room table

9. Rules

10. Allowance

11. Family recipes

12. Grandparents

13. Reunions

14. Cousins

15. Video game time

16. Pet dog

17. Favorite chair

18. Trash day

19. Stepparents

20. Adoption

21. Good listener

22. Baby dedication

23. Pet cat

24. Family pictures

25. Christmas tradition

26. Family car

27. Babysitting

28. Grocery trips

29. Service projects

30. Uncle

31. Aunt

32. Godparents

33. Car trouble

34. Change

35. Apartment living

36. Photo albums

37. Wedding

38. Easter Sunday

39. Mailbox

40. Refrigerator magnets

41. Bedroom

42. Sister

43. Brother

44. Game night

45. Community Service

46. TV shows

47. Garage sales

48. New baby

49. Cell phone bill

50. Bibles

51. Family videos

52. Easter tradition

NONESSENTIALS | CULTURE OPPOSITES

IT'S OPꟼOSITE DAY.

In this chapter you'll get your group sharing opposite about things they'll encounter in our culture. After you've explained how sharing opposite works and you've declared it Opposite Day, you'll start the discussion with the words listed in this chapter. Ask each student to respond to the word you provide. Say: "In a sentence or two, tell how you feel about _____ (but not really)." After everyone has had a chance to share, or after a few rounds, you will need to formally end Opposite Day. Be sure to leave a few minutes to share what you learned about each other.

1. MP3 players

2. Energy drinks

3. Skate parks

4. Social networking sites

5. Study abroad

6. Playlists

7. Swimming pools

8. Boy bands

9. Broadway musicals

10. Free hugs

11. Anime

12. Blogging

13. Video editing

14. Fashion week

15. Web design

16. Knitting

17. Snowboarding

18. Paintball

19. Smart phones

20. College football

21. Talent competitions

22. Environmental concern

23. Sudoku

24. World travel

25. Joining a cause

26. The mall

27. MTV

28. Surfing

29. Guitar lessons

30. Thanksgiving Day football

31. Digital self-portraits

32. The Nobel Peace Prize

33. The Olympic Games

34. Triathlons

35. Video chat

36. Makeover shows

37. Soda

38. Wi-Fi

39. Hotdog-eating contests

40. Celebrity playlists

41. <u>The New York Times</u>

42. Daylight saving time

43. Independent movies

44. Stock exchanges

45. Hybrid cars

46. Art museums

47. Premium coffee

48. DVR

49. Public transportation

50. The History Channel

51. Public forums

52. Music festivals

SYSTEMATIC I RANDOM OPPOSITES

IT'S OPPOSITE DAY.

This chapter brings some random stuff to enlighten your opposite brains. After you've explained how sharing opposite works and you've declared it Opposite Day, you'll start the discussion with the words listed in this chapter. Ask each student to respond to the random word you provide. Say: "In a sentence or two, tell how you feel about _____ (but not really)." After everyone has had a chance to share, or after a few rounds, you will need to formally end Opposite Day. Be sure to leave a few minutes to share what you learned about each other.

1. Hurricanes

2. Tortilla chips

3. Chia Pets

4. Lava lamps

5. Leeches

6. Super bouncy balls

7. Mariachi bands

8. Sushi

9. Donut holes

10. Car air fresheners

11. Chipmunks

12. Driftwood

13. Bobsleds

14. Guinea pigs

15. Four square

16. Hibachi

17. Convertibles

18. Flip flops

19. Athlete's foot

20. Friday nights

21. Spinach dip

22. Parakeets

23. Motorcycles

24. Weight training

25. Haunted houses

26. Palm trees

27. Pizza delivery

28. Snowdrifts

29. Podcasting

30. Scented candles

31. HDTV

32. Converse shoes

33. *Street ball*

34. *Skipping rocks*

35. *Piercings*

36. *Mohawks*

37. *Legos*

38. *Origami*

39. Ski lifts

40. Bloody noses

41. Leap years

42. Birthmarks

43. Caves

44. Scuba diving

45. Subways

46. Sporks

47. Wooden roller coasters

48. Dentists

49. S'mores

50. Racetracks

51. Sasquatch

52. Pop-Tarts

SHRINKING | GROWING UP OPPOSITES

IT'S OPPOSITE DAY.

Today you get to share opposite about things you might run into as a person grows up. After you've explained how sharing opposite works and you've declared it Opposite Day, you'll start the discussion with the words listed in this chapter. Ask each student to respond to the word you provide. Say: "In a sentence or two, tell how you feel about _____ (but not really)." After everyone has had a chance to share, or after a few rounds, you will need to formally end Opposite Day. Be sure to leave a few minutes to share what you learned about each other.

1. Morning cartoons

2. Educational toys

3. Learner's permit

4. Driving test

5. First job

6. Career shadowing

7. ABCs

8. Shoe tying

9. Ice cream trucks

10. Swim floaties

11. Bike riding

12. Training wheels

13. Pizza rolls

14. Sleepovers

15. Night-lights

16. Room sharing

17. Responsibility

18. Internet safety

19. Immunizations

20. Sports teams

21. Parent coaches

22. Strep throat

23. Christmas lists

24. Jell-O

25. New shoes

26. Confirmation

27. Easter egg hunts

28. Family road trips

29. Feet pajamas

30. Mom time

31. Dad time

32. Chill time

33. 15th birthday

34. Sweet 16

35. Adulthood

36. College applications

37. Car pools

38. Youth group graduation

39. Senior pictures

40. Volunteer hours

41. School agendas

42. Growing pains

43. Baby teeth

44. Growth spurts

45. Decisions

46. Roommates

47. Savings accounts

48. Personal mission

49. Fiancé(e)

50. Master's degree

51. Mission trips

52. Photo albums

UNFAMILIARITY | FAMILY OPPOSITES

It's time to talk about literal opposites. In this chapter, no one needs to declare it Opposite Day. Ask each group member to share one or two sentences about these opposite things in their lives. The opposites are found in the nature of the descriptions this time around (and not in the responses). Be sure to make this clear if you've done a previous Opposite Day chapter in the same setting.

1. Youngest family member and oldest family member

2. The place you lived when you were born and the place you live now

3. *Favorite and least favorite dwelling space*

4. *Most predictable family member and most spontaneous family member*

5. *The giver and the tightwad in the family (no names, please)*

6. *Most stylish and least stylish member*

7. *Best and worst vacation locations*

8. *Happiest and saddest moments experienced as a family*

9. Blandest and tastiest home-cooked meals

10. Funniest and scariest moments at a family reunion

11. Best and worst road trip

12. Junkiest and nicest family car

13. A recent worthwhile conversation and a ridiculous argument

14. Most memorable vacation and one you'd like to be erased in time

15. *Least favorite family chore and most enjoyable family project*

16. *A crazy over-scheduled day and a restful day together*

17. *Weirdest and coolest guests*

18. *Funniest church pew moment and most serious church pew moment*

19. *A time when you were late as a family and a time when you were early*

20. *Most patient family member and least patient*

21. Best birthday party and most disastrous birthday party

22. Most excellent family picture and one you never share

23. Nastiest for real flu and a time when you weren't really that sick

24. The one you can tell anything and the one you dare not share secrets with

25. The planner and the player

26. The prankster and the rule follower

27. The quiet one and the screamer

28. The coordinated and the clumsy

29. The hyper and the chill

30. Greatest way to make mom (or caregiver) happy and the best way to frustrate her (or him)

31. Finest glass in the cupboard and the most family-friendly glass in the cupboard

32. The guest dishes versus the everyday dishes

33. Favored seat in the house and the place no one sits

34. Most useful thing in the garage and most useless thing in the garage

35. Finest piece of art in the house and most ridiculous piece of art in the house

36. Cousin you know well and a cousin whose name you forget

37. Favorite family board game and lamest family board game

38. Top Christmas memory and bottom Christmas memory

39. Top Christmas gift and bottom Christmas gift

40. Enthusiastic family agreement on something and a forced parental decision

41. Good church memory and an unpleasant church memory

42. Sibling (or cousin) most like you and least like you

43. How you best resemble your mom and how you least resemble your mom

44. Strongest resemblance to your dad and weakest resemblance

45. *Favorite family TV show and the show you wish you could turn off*

46. *Movie everyone agreed to watch and one that no one wanted to see*

47. *Top restaurant choice and bottom restaurant choice*

48. *Comfiest family blanket and itchiest*

49. *Quickest chore and most laborious chore*

50. *Most vivid family memory and the dullest*

51. One moment you wish you could relive as a family and one you wish you could forget

52. The most peaceful and most chaotic Thanksgiving you've spent together

SECONDARY | EDUCATION OPPOSITES

It's time to talk about literal opposites you might find at school. In this chapter, no one needs to declare it Opposite Day. Ask each group member to respond by giving details about each of the opposites listed below. The opposites are found in the nature of the descriptions this time around (and not in the responses). Make sure to make this clear if you've done a previous Opposite Day chapter in the same setting.

1. Most exciting book you've ever read and the lamest

2. Favorite gym class memory and one you would rather not relive

3. Best elementary school teacher and worst

4. An emergency situation and a false alarm

5. Funniest lunchroom story and most pathetic lunchroom story

6. Easiest grade you earned and the grade you worked for the hardest

7. Most dramatic national event this year and the one everyone forgot in a day

8. Teacher you wish you could replace and a teacher you wish you could have longer

9. Best college and worst college

10. A day with information overload and a day of rest

11. Earliest childhood memory and the most recent memory

12. An assignment you disliked and an assignment you enjoyed

13. Clothes you liked and clothes you wished you could "lose"

14. A time when you were late and a time when you were early

15. An enjoyable fundraiser and one that felt like torture

16. Lamest school party and coolest school party

17. Elementary school bus ride vs. middle school bus ride

18. Moment when you should have stood up for what was right and a moment when you did

19. Favorite career day career and least favorite career day career

20. A sweet science fair project and a stupid science fair project

21. Language you would like to learn and one you're not interested in

22. Longest test ever and shortest test ever

23. Quickest school assembly and longest

24. Best awards ceremony and worst awards ceremony

25. Type of friend you hope to have until graduation and type of friend you hope to stay away from

26. ADD teacher and super-organized teacher

27. Class you fell asleep in and a class that's impossible to fall asleep in

28. Coolest field trip and most useless field trip

29. Walking home or parent pickup

30. Classic literature or contemporary fiction

31. Incredible school play and one that made you feel sorry for the cast

32. Sickest dissection (think science class) and most interesting dissection

33. Earliest wake-up time and latest wake-up time

34. Busiest summer and chillest summer

35. A home economics disaster and home economics masterpiece

36. Something you look forward to next year and something you want to remember from last year

37. Something you're dreading about next year and something you dreaded about last year

38. Friend with the sloppiest handwriting and friend with the neatest handwriting

39. Best group project and worst group project

40. A picture you would like to have framed and a picture you wish would be destroyed

41. Most annoying sound at school and most pleasant sound at school

42. Awesome grade school haircut and most tragic haircut

43. Diligent homework buddy and one who gets distracted

44. Longest standardized test and the shortest

45. Strictest substitute teacher and most flexible

46. Favorite lunch box or bag and the one you "accidentally" left at school

47. Sweetest Christmas play and most insufferable

48. Exciting spring break and most dreary

49. Supreme classroom party and the most measly

50. Most gratifying community service hours and most squandered community service hours (time well spent and time wasted)

51. Something you wish you could take back and something you would do over again if given the chance

52. First day of school and last day of school

CONTACTS I FRIENDSHIP OPPOSITES

Don't declare it Opposite Day in this chapter, but give everyone a chance to think about the different types of friends they have.

This section isn't meant to be a popularity contest or a simple list of superlatives. It's meant to launch discussion about the myriad of friends a person can have, some opposite in personality and some much the same. Have group members complete the sentence with a name and share why that person is the answer for them.

Share your friend opposites by completing the sentence.

1. The friend I would rather have lunch at the mall with is...

2. My friend who is most committed to her faith is...

3. The friend I can be myself with is...

4. The most athletic friend I have is...

5. The friend I could see myself being friends with after high school is...

6. My most loyal friend is...

7. The friend who can text message the fastest is...

8. My friend who loves sports the most is...

9. The best shopping partner is...

10. My friend who could ride a skateboard all day long is...

11. My craziest friend is...

12. The friend who writes really well is...

13. The friend who has the most natural talent is...

14. My friend who wears whatever he wants and doesn't really care is...

15. The friend who smells the cleanest is...

16. My friend who can keep a secret is...

17. A friend I try not to be jealous of is...

18. My most tech-savvy friend is...

19. The most artistic friend I know is...

20. The most daring friend I have is...

21. My most creative friend is...

22. My friend who is most likely to start a business is...

23. My most compassionate friend is...

24. The friend I have who is the bravest is...

25. My friend who will eat anything is...

26. My friend who dresses most like me is...

27. The friend who is most kindhearted is...

28. The friend who needs the least amount of sleep is...

29. My most environmentally minded friend is...

30. My most reliable friend is...

31. The friend who always has my back is...

32. The friend I talk to most on the phone is...

33. The friend who is most likely to attend an Ivy League school is...

34. The friend I would most like to take a vacation with is...

35. My most random friend is...

36. My funniest friend is...

37. The friend I could see becoming the president of the United States is...

38. My friend who has the most style is...

39. The friend whose family I would like to be a part of is...

40. My most unpredictable friend is...

41. My most organized friend is...

42. The friend who most personifies a servant is...

43. The friend who listens best is...

44. My best gaming friend is...

45. My friend with the best taste in music is...

46. The most likely to become zookeeper is...

47. The most spontaneous friend I have is...

48. My friend who is most dedicated to her parents is...

49. My friend who can make the craziest faces is...

50. The friend who is most involved in his church youth group is...

51. The friend most likely to end up in the Olympics is...

52. My friend who will always keep me accountable is...

DISPLACEMENT I LOCATION OPPOSITES

Learn about each other's climate and living preferences by looking at these opposites together. Have students choose which location opposite fits them best. Make sure to tell your group that it's not an official Opposite Day response time. This chapter is more about picking your favorite opposite with the group. If there's time, give people the chance to share why they picked one opposite over another.

1. Beach house or mountain cabin

2. Tent or four-star hotel

3. Zoo or museum

4. Apartment living or house living

5. Flat in Manhattan or ranch house in Arizona

6. East coast or west coast

7. City or country

8. Hammock or air mattress

9. Historic bungalow or newest design

10. Wood floors or carpet

11. Scenic or city view

12. World's largest city or world's smallest village

13. Temporary housing or permanent residence

14. Mud hut or concrete walls

15. Clothes dryer or clothesline

16. Modern art or vintage art

17. Sepia tone or color

18. Mailbox or post office

19. Inside dog or outside dog

20. Shelves of books or shelves of DVDs

21. Super tidy or super messy

22. Stainless steel or pearly white

23. Cloth or leather

24. Alone or with roommates

25. Fake plants or real plants

26. Hand wash or dishwasher

27. On the stove or grill outside

28. Mansion or modest

29. Lakeside or poolside

30. New or thrift store-bought

31. Natural or fluorescent lighting

32. Top or bottom floor

33. Cottage or trailer

34. Single or double-wide

35. Open windows or darkened shades

36. Dry weather or humid weather

37. Igloo or tiki hut

38. Guard dog or alarm system

39. Over 100 years old or brand new

40. PC house or Mac house

41. Basement or attic

42. Gym membership or home equipment

43. Backyard or no yard

44. Satellite TV or no TV

45. Busy street or quiet street

46. Recycle or throw away

47. Mega Christmas lights or few decorations

48. Shoes at door or shoes can go anywhere

49. Unidentifiable food in fridge or fresh food only

50. By the beach or by the mountains

51. Swing on the porch or recliner in the house

52. Flowers in pots or weeds in the yard

WEAR IT OUT | FASHION OPPOSITES

I'm not very adventurous when it comes to personal style. I stick to the basics: Colored tanks and jeans are my staples. On a random day you might catch me doing something fashionably stupid like wearing three inch, pointy toe, brown suede high heels to the theater. Not only do they look obtuse, but they also make me high-step like a drum major and get caught in tiny cracks and crevices causing me to stumble to new ankle-twisting heights—stuff like that can seriously kill you! Shoes like those might just be as nonsensical as skinny jeans so small your feet get stuck in them...or wearing plastic to lose weight during wrestling practice—leaving guys dehydrated and dizzy. Whatever it is, some of us are willing to pay the price.

Some of us are usually up for a dare or willing to try something different when it comes to fashion. Here you get to share how far you would go with some style opposites—if given the chance.

The phrases "I would wear it" and "I wouldn't wear it" are your guiding opposite responses for this section.

Give your group the chance to answer this question as their Opposite Day exercise: Is this style an opposite for you? Answer either "wear it" or "wouldn't wear it." Then tell us why! This isn't a traditional Opposite Day sharing chapter—your responses should be straightforward here.

1. The color pink

2. Pleather

3. Turtlenecks

4. Christmas vest (with tiny reindeer)

5. All black

6. Cowboy hat

7. Hockey jersey

8. Giant "bling" necklaces

9. Black liquid eyeliner

10. Tie-dye

11. Peace signs

12. Anything with your rival team's logo

13. Combat boots

14. An all-white tuxedo

15. Ear gauges

16. Duct tape

17. Hair extensions

18. Animal fur

19. Thrift-store finds

20. Big glasses

21. Skinny jeans

22. Wide-leg flare jeans

23. College football jacket

24. Knee socks

25. A kilt

26. Wet suit

27. Hula skirt

28. Zebra pants

29. Wool cardigan

30. Jean jacket

31. Sombrero

32. Baseball jersey

33. Formal dress

34. Mohawk

35. Cape

36. Kimono

37. Rain boots

38. Camouflage

39. Mullet

40. Biker pants

41. Big hair

42. Shoulder pads

43. Kid T-shirts

44. Platform shoes

45. Feather boas

46. Plaid

47. Oversized shades

48. Moccasin boots

49. Cutoff T-shirts

50. Self-tanning lotion

51. Boat shoes

52. Snowsuit

FLIPSIDE | JESUS OPPOSITES

Throughout the New Testament, Jesus teaches by example. His style wasn't what the world had been waiting for, and it felt foreign to most (including the religious leaders). His ways still feel foreign to us because they defy our instincts to watch out for *numero uno* and to create our own personal wealth and happiness. Jesus' teachings, if we'll let them, have the ability to transform our minds to see as he would.

As a group, find the opposite call in each message. These are the Bible's red letters—words straight from Jesus, the author of opposite. Talk about how each sentence calls us to live differently. Talk to each other about how life might look different if you lived by these instructions. It may be a good idea to talk about a Jesus opposite at the end of each *Opposite Day* response time. These words offer us a chance to live beyond opposite, to live a third way—the way of Christ.

Scripture from *The Message Remix* unless otherwise noted

1. Matthew 5:3
You're blessed when you're at the end of your rope. With less of you there is more of God and his rule.

2. Matthew 5:4
You're blessed when you feel you've lost what is most dear to you. Only then can you be embraced by the One most dear to you.

3. Matthew 5:5
You're blessed when you're content with just who you are—no more, no less. That's the moment you find yourselves proud owners of everything that can't be bought.

4. Matthew 5:10
You're blessed when your commitment to God provokes persecution. The persecution drives you even deeper into God's kingdom.

5. Matthew 5:11-12
Not only that—count yourselves blessed every time people put you down or throw you out or speak lies about you to discredit me. What it means is that the truth is too close for comfort and they are uncomfortable. You can be glad when that happens— give a cheer, even!—for though they don't like it, I do! And all heaven applauds. And know that you are in good company. My prophets and witnesses have always gotten into this kind of trouble.

6. Matthew 5:39-42

Here's what I propose: "Don't hit back at all." If someone strikes you, stand there and take it. If someone drags you into court and sues for the shirt off your back, giftwrap your best coat and make a present of it. And if someone takes unfair advantage of you, use the occasion to practice the servant life. No more tit-for-tat stuff. Live generously.

7. Matthew 5:43-45 (Luke 6:27, Romans 12:20) TNIV

You have heard that it was said, "Love your neighbor and hate your enemy." But I tell you, love your enemies and pray for those who persecute you, that you may be children of your Father in heaven.

8. Matthew 6:19-21

Don't hoard treasure down here where it gets eaten by moths and corroded by rust or—worse!—stolen by burglars. Stockpile treasure in heaven, where it's safe from moth and rust and burglars. It's obvious, isn't it? The place where your treasure is, is the place you will most want to be, and end up being.

9. Matthew 7:13-14

Don't look for shortcuts to God. The market is flooded with surefire, easygoing formulas for a successful life that can be practiced in your spare time. Don't fall for that stuff, even though crowds of people do. The way to life—to God!—is vigorous and requires total attention.

10. Matthew 10:39 (Luke 9:24, Luke 17:33)

If your first concern is to look after yourself, you'll never find yourself. But if you forget about yourself and look to me, you'll find both yourself and me.

11. Matthew 11:29-30 (1 John 5:3; how can a yoke be easy?)

Walk with me and work with me—watch how I do it. Learn the unforced rhythms of grace. I won't lay anything heavy or ill-fitting on you. Keep company with me and you'll learn to live freely and lightly.

12. Matthew 16:25 (Mark 8:35, John 12:25) TNIV

For whoever wants to save their life will lose it, but whoever loses their life for me will find it.

13. Matthew 18:4 TNIV
Therefore, whoever takes a humble place—becoming like this child—is the greatest in the kingdom of heaven.

14. Matthew 19:30 (Matthew 20:16, Mark 10:31, Luke 13:30)
This is the Great Reversal: many of the first ending up last, and the last first.

15. Matthew 20:26-28 (Mark 10:43, Luke 22:26)
Whoever wants to be great must become a servant. Whoever wants to be first among you must be your slave. That is what the Son of Man has done: He came to serve, not be served—and then to give away his life in exchange for the many who are held hostage.

16. Matthew 21:31-32 TNIV

Truly I tell you, the tax collectors and the prostitutes are entering the kingdom of God ahead of you. For John came to you to show you the way of righteousness, and you did not believe him, but the tax collectors and the prostitutes did. And even after you saw this, you did not repent and believe him.

17. Matthew 23:12 (Luke 14:11) TNIV

For those who exalt themselves will be humbled, and those who humble themselves will be exalted.

18. Luke 6:35-36

I tell you, love your enemies. Help and give without expecting a return. You'll never—I promise—regret it. Live out this God-created identity the way our Father lives toward us, generously and graciously, even when we're at our worst. Our Father is kind; you be kind.

19. Luke 13:30 TNIV
Indeed there are those who are last who will be first, and first who will be last.

20. Luke 14:10-11
When you're invited to dinner, go and sit at the last place. Then when the host comes he may very well say, "Friend, come up to the front." That will give the dinner guests something to talk about! What I'm saying is, If you walk around with your nose in the air, you're going to end up flat on your face. But if you're content to be simply yourself, you will become more than yourself.

21. John 11:25-26

You don't have to wait for the End. I am, right now, Resurrection and Life. The one who believes in me, even though he or she dies, will live. And everyone who lives believing in me does not ultimately die at all. Do you believe this?

22. John 12:25-26 TNIV

Those who love their life will lose it, while those who hate their life in this world will keep it for eternal life. Whoever serves me must follow me; and where I am, my servant also will be. My Father will honor the one who serves me.

23. John 20:15-17 TNIV

He asked her, "Woman, why are you crying? Who is it you are looking for?" Thinking he was the gardener, she said, "Sir, if you have carried him away, tell me where you have put him, and I will get him." Jesus said to her, "Mary." She turned toward him and cried out in Aramaic, "Rabboni!" (which means "Teacher"). Jesus said, "Do not hold on to me, for I have not yet ascended to the Father. Go instead to my brothers and tell them, 'I am ascending to my Father and your Father, to my God and your God.'"

24. Acts 20:35 TNIV
It is more blessed to give than to receive.

THE OPPOSITE DAY CHALLENGE

Go even deeper:

In these stories told by Jesus you'll find a way of living paralleled by no other—and that makes it opposite to our normal, knee-jerk way of life. Jesus said, "I am the way, the truth, and the life." If we believe this is true, we should look into this alternative way of living and maybe even adopt it as "the way" for us.

1. Luke 10:30-36—The opposite way of the Samaritan

2. Luke 10:38-42—The opposite way of Mary

3. Luke 21:1-4—The opposite way of the widow

4. Luke 23:34—The opposite ways of Jesus

5. Luke 8:1-15—The opposite ways of Jesus

6. John 12:1-8—The opposite mind of Mary

7. John 15:13 (John 10:11, Romans 5:7-8)—The opposite way

8. 2 Corinthians 12:8-10—The power of opposite

Opposite Day comes to us by way of children's street culture. It's a game children play together. It's often spontaneous and needs little explanation. There have been a few portrayals of the phenomenon of Opposite Day on television, and many shows like to play off of its humor. There are two shows that have made an impression on me (and by impression I mean these shows made me laugh and made me want to play, too!). So check out these short bird's-eye views into Opposite Day and allow the culture to sink in as you share.

REVERSE LAND I TV & MUSIC OPPOSITES
(IDEAS TO ILLUSTRATE THE POINT)

Use these TV episodes to get your group in the mood for sharing opposite. Both episodes are hilarious. It's fun to watch the characters figure out how to behave on Opposite Day. And it will be equally hilarious to watch each other! (Please preview the content of the *Seinfeld* episode before showing it to young people.)

SpongeBob SquarePants
Episode: "Opposite Day"
Season 1 (First Aired: September 11, 1999)

Summary: Squidward is fed up with his neighbors SpongeBob and Patrick and calls a realtor for his house to be sold. He's told there should be no problem selling his house as long as it's in good condition and not surrounded by bad neighbors or something. Knowing that SpongeBob and Patrick are likely to ruin his chances of selling his house, he comes up with a plan.

Squidward convinces SpongeBob that it's Opposite Day—the one day of the year when you get to behave differently. SpongeBob starts the day out mildly by staying in bed and being in a bad mood. However, he and Patrick take the day to a new level when they start pretending to be Squidward and by a chain of opposite events end up thwarting the sale of his house.

TALKING POINTS:

1. Let's say today is Opposite Day. What type of person would be the opposite of you?

2. Have you ever played a game that went drastically wrong? Did anyone get hurt?

3. What would be one drawback of having to live "opposite"?

4. What would be one advantage of living "opposite"?

Seinfeld
Episode: "The Opposite"
Season 5 (First Aired: May 19, 1994)

Summary: In this episode, George is desperate and concludes every instinct and decision he's ever made in life has been wrong. He haphazardly decides to do the opposite from now on. As George starts his opposite behavior (ordering a different meal, saying what's on his mind, etc.), his sore luck changes. You see him finally get a girl, a new job, and independence as he moves out of his parents' home. Things start to get unlucky for Elaine, who uncharacteristically gets kicked out of her apartment and loses her job. The end of the episode shows Elaine sulking in the restaurant booth with Jerry. She feels like George!

TALKING POINTS:

1. What would happen if you decided to do everything opposite like George did? What things in your life would go from bad to good? Good to bad?

2. It's easy to get stuck in a routine. How does George's "opposite religion" change his life?

3. In this episode, Jerry is "even Steven." He believes that everything has a way of balancing out: George gets a house, and Elaine loses her house. Do you think life has a way of balancing out? Or is it just by chance you get certain opportunities and miss out on others?

4. What are some behaviors or habits you could pick up right now that will help you live your dreams like George did?

5. What are some ways you can change your routine to make time for the God who created you and gave you those dreams?

JUST FOR FUN

There are a number of Opposite Day songs and skits from *Sesame Street*. The one with the mnah-mnah puppet is a crowd favorite. http://www.sesamestreet.org/videos

An amazing set of songs for your playlist (and other useful opposite stuff):
Album: *Opposite Way* | Leeland
http://leelandonline.com/oppositeway/main

What if Opposite Day were an online holiday?
1. Describe your opposite MySpace or Facebook profile.
2. How often would you check your email?
3. Would you add or delete friends on that day?
4. Would you blog more or less?
5. Would texting on your cell phone increase or decrease?

Opposite Game
Play a version of act-it-out tag where two or three people act out a scenario you've given them (like driving a go-cart or playing dodgeball). At spontaneous moments during the game any member of the group can call out "PAUSE!" The group member who called out the pause must then take the place of one of the players and begin to act out a different scenario (they might say something like, "It sure is fun collecting eggs during the Easter egg hunt").

It's fun to watch when the group is pretending to play dodgeball and they are switched into a different scenario quickly—like hunting for Easter eggs. To make this game fun for Opposite Day, have the players act how they normally wouldn't. If the scenario calls for a high intensity set of movements (for example, karate at youth group), then they would act lethargic—interpreting the game through an Opposite Day mindset.

Provide a few chairs and maybe even a few props for this game. You can decide scenarios beforehand or allow the players to make them up as they go. Set some guidelines for rowdy groups (no headlocks, ankle-biting, stuff like that).